DEC   2001

DATE DUE

Volcanoes of the World™

Kilauea
Hawaii's Most Active
Volcano

Kathy Furgang

The Rosen Publishing Group's
PowerKids Press™
New York

For Michael

Published in 2001 by The Rosen Publishing Group, Inc.
29 East 21st Street, New York, NY 10010

First Edition

Series and Book Design: Michael Caroleo

Photo Credits: p.1 © Michael T. Sedam/CORBIS; p. 4 © Neil Rabinowitz/CORBIS; pp. 6-7 (illustration) by Michael Caroleo; pp. 8, 15 © Roger Ressmeyer/CORBIS; pp. 11, 19 © CORBIS; p.12 (background Hawaii) © Richard A. Cooke/CORBIS; p. 12 (goddess Pele image) © Robert Holmes/CORBIS; p. 16 © James L. Amos/CORBIS; p. 20 © Douglas Peebles/CORBIS; p.21 Photodisc.

Furgang, Kathy.
    Mt. Kilauea : Hawaii's most active volcano / by Kathy Furgang.
        p. cm.— (Volcanoes of the world)
    Includes index.
    Summary: Describes the formation of the Hawaiian islands and the continuing eruptions of Mt. Kilauea.
    ISBN 0-8239-5659-8 (alk. paper)
    1. Kilauea Volcano (Hawaii)—Juvenile literature. 2. Volcanism—Hawaii—Juvenile literature. [Kilauea Volcano (Hawaii) 2. Volcanoes.] I. Title: Mt. Kilauea. II.Title.

    QE523.K5 F87 2000
    551.21'09969'1—dc21   00-020880

Manufactured in the United States of America

Contents

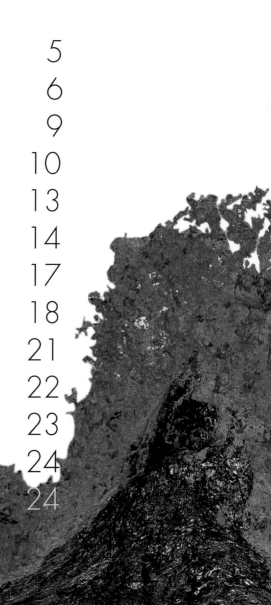

The island of Hawaii is the home of Kilauea, which is shown here at sunset.

Hawaii, Islands of Beauty

Hawaii is one of the most beautiful states in America. This state is really eight islands in the Pacific Ocean. Hawaii has warm weather, wonderful mountains, green plants, and tropical beaches. Other features that make Hawaii beautiful are its mighty volcanoes. Each island has at least one volcano. Most of the volcanoes are not active. The main island of Hawaii has two active volcanoes called Kilauea and Mauna Loa. The giant volcano Kilauea bubbles and spits out red-hot liquid rock almost every day. The Hawaiian people who have lived near this powerful force of nature for years are used to it. Kilauea has attracted visitors from all around the world.

A Volcano Is Born

A volcano is a break in Earth's surface. Hot, liquid rock from far below the ground pours out of it. This liquid is called **magma**. Earth is made up of three layers. We live on the top layer. This layer is called the **crust**. It is made of solid rock. Underneath the crust is a layer of solid and liquid rock called the **mantle**. The third layer is the **core**. The core is the very center of Earth. It is made of extremely hot solid and liquid iron. The entire mantle is heated by the core. A volcano forms when magma from Earth's mantle shoots through a break in the crust and reaches the surface.

Mantle

Core

Crust

Earth's crust is 5 to 25 miles (8 to 40 km) thick. Its mantle is about 1,800 miles (2,900 km) thick. The core of Earth is 2,150 miles (3,460 km) across.

Steam rises as hot lava from Kilauea pours into the Pacific Ocean.
When lava cools, it hardens into rock.

Kilauea Is One Hot Spot!

It takes Earth thousands, and sometimes millions of years to make a volcano. Earth's crust is made of large sections called **plates**. The plates are moving all the time, even though we can't feel them. They move very slowly, only a few inches (cm) each year. Many volcanoes form when plates push into each other and crack the crust. Kilauea, however, was formed by a hot spot. When bubbles of hot magma break through the center of a plate, they create a hot spot. Magma from the mantle shoots up through the hot spot. This action is called an **eruption**. We use the word **lava** to describe magma that has reached Earth's crust. After hot lava erupts, it then cools and hardens into solid rock.

9

The Story of Hawaii

Millions of years ago, the area where Hawaii now stands was nothing but ocean. Each Hawaiian island was formed, one at a time, from the same hot spot on the ocean floor. Volcanoes that begin on the ocean floor are called **submarine volcanoes**. Lava builds up to form rock. New eruptions cause lava to build and harden on top of the old lava. When the hardened lava reaches out of the ocean, an island is created. Earth's plates keep moving all the time, but hot spots rarely move. Moving plates caused the first Hawaiian island to move off of the hot spot. That volcano no longer erupted. A new volcano was formed in place of the old one. This volcano also became one of Hawaii's islands.

This is a view of the Hawiian islands from high in the sky.
Each island has at least one volcano.

This is an image of the mythical goddess Pele. Some people in Hawaii believe that giving offerings to Pele will prevent dangerous eruptions.

Pele, Goddess of Fire

A myth is a story that is told and retold over time. The Hawaiian people tell the myth that volcanoes were controlled by Pele, the goddess of fire. They believe that Pele, the daughter of the Earth Mother and Sky Father, used volcanoes to burn lands, melt rocks, and to punish and kill people who did not obey her. She would sometimes appear to people as a beautiful young girl and sometimes as an old woman. Hawaiians say that Pele has lived in each of the Hawaiian volcanoes. Her cruel older sister, the goddess of the sea, drove her out of each volcano. Each time Pele was forced to make her home in a new volcano. Some people still believe that Pele now lives in Kilauea.

Science and Volcanoes

Today most people do not use myths to explain powerful forces of nature. Now scientists know a lot about volcanoes and how they form. These scientists are called **volcanologists**. The study of volcanoes is called **volcanology**. Volcanologists can even predict when a volcano will erupt next. They use special tools that tell them when areas of Earth are moving. One tool is called a **seismometer**. This tool measures Earth's movements. A seismometer can tell when an **earthquake** might happen. When plates under an area of Earth move and shake, that may also mean a volcano in that region will erupt soon.

The scientist examining the hot lava pool on Kilauea is a volcanologist.

The photo shows footsteps left in cooled black lava. The Kilauea volcano is in the background.

Kilauea's Very Large Neighbor

Kilauea rises over 4,000 feet (1,219 m) above the sea. It is actually located on the slope of an even bigger volcanic mountain called Mauna Loa. Mauna Loa is about 10,000 feet (3,048 m) higher than the top of Kilauea. Both volcanoes erupt, but Kilauea erupts almost every day. Kilauea is a shield volcano. These volcanoes are called shield volcanoes because they are shaped like ancient Greek shields. From an airplane, Kilauea might also look like a bowl turned upside down. Lava pours out from a single **vent**. It collects in a **caldera**, or bowl-shaped crater. Then the lava on Kilauea streams down the mountain in many directions.

A Powerful History

The crater inside Kilauea is called Halemaumau. For about a hundred years there was a giant, hot, bubbling lake of lava inside this crater. In 1924, an amazing thing happened. The lake of lava sank and disappeared from sight. Then a terrible eruption of steam took place. From that point on, Kilauea started to erupt more and more often. The longest running cycle of eruptions started in 1983. The volcano bubbles out about 500,000 cubic yards (382,277 cu m) of lava every day. By 1995, cooled lava flows had added about 500 acres (2.02 sq km) of new land to the island.

Smoke rises from the center of Kilauea's Halemaumau crater.

The lava flow from Kilauea is slow enough to allow people to safely watch.

Eruption!

In 1989, lava poured from Kilauea after an eruption. It ruined a visitor's center in the Hawaii Volcanoes National Park. By the next year, 65 houses had been destroyed by mighty Kilauea. Lava flows slowly covered streets, killing plants and wildlife that got in the way. Most of the time, people are given plenty of notice so they can get out of the way of Kilauea's lava flows. In fact, millions of people visit Hawaii so that they can see the volcano in action. The lava flows from Kilauea slowly, so people can watch from a distance without being in danger.

New Islands on the Way

Will Pele, the goddess of fire, one day move to a new volcano like the Hawaiian myth says? Will her cruel sister, the goddess of the sea, chase her away from her home? Kilauea is the youngest volcano of the Hawaiian islands, but it will not be the youngest forever. A new Hawaiian island is being formed right now, but it has not yet reached above the surface of the ocean. The oldest of the volcanic islands have sunk back into the sea. The ocean wears down the rock and the islands sink under the water. Volcanoes are changing the way Earth looks. Hawaii and Kilauea continue to change every day.

Glossary

caldera (kal-DEHR-ah) A crater formed by a volcano.

core (KOR) The hot center of Earth that is made of liquid and solid iron.

crust (KRUST) Earth's top layer of solid rock on which we live.

earthquake (URTH-kwayk) The shaking or trembling of Earth's crust due to the movement of large pieces of land called plates running into each other.

eruption (ih-RUP-shun) The explosion of gases, smoke, ash, and lava from a volcano.

lava (LAH-vuh) Magma that has reached Earth's crust and hardened into rock.

magma (MAG-muh) Hot liquid rock found in the mantle of Earth.

mantle (MAN-tuhl) The layer of Earth that lies between the core and crust of Earth's surface.

plates (PLAYTS) Large sections of Earth's crust that move and shift over time.

seismometer (syz-MAH-meh-ter) An instrument used to measure the movement of Earth.

submarine volcanoes (sub-mahr-EEHN vol-KAY-noz) Volcanoes that begin on the ocean floor.

vent (VENT) A hole or opening that serves as an outlet.

volcanology (vol-kuh-NOL-uh-jee) The study of volcanoes.

volcanologists (vol-kuh-NOL-uh-jists) People who study volcanoes.

Index

Web Sites

To learn more about Kilauea, volcanoes, and Hawaii, visit these Web sites:

http://tqjunior.advanced.org/5410/
http://wwwhvo.wr.usgs.gov/kilauea/update/main.html
http://volcano.und.edu/

24